Adult Coloring Book
Auntie V.'s Vintage Vault
Grannie's Scarves

V. PEREIRA

Adult Coloring Book
Auntie V.'s Vintage Vault
Grannies Scarves

ISBN-13: 978-1530033256

ISBN-10: 153003325X

DEDICATIONS

For Great Grandma Sally (Odessa) Ashby, and Mama Clairice Hegwood.

But most of all, to my sister Sandy.

Love you to the moon and back, Sister!

Do you remember the soft, silky, colorful scarfs that
belonged to your grandmother.
You know, the slippery squares of patterned material that
moms every where, folded away for safe keeping?
Hidden deep in the bottom of an undergarment drawer,
or tucked away in the Hope Chest,
or even hanging on a scarve hanger in the closet.
Those scarves have always held a place of intrigue in my mind.

When my sister Sandy and I would play dress-up,we would
beg our mom to bring out her grandmother's silk scarves.
We would tie them around our heads, then fold them corner
 to corner and place them around our shoulders like a shawl.

We would wrap them around our wrists, and stuff them in the necks
of our shirts to look like big ties. We'd make bows out of them and
pin them to our clothes. We'd make shirts and skirts and hats out of
them and wear them across our face like in 'I Dream of Jeanie'.

We were princesses and paupers.

Mothers and Grannies.

Mary Anne and Ginger.

I fondly remember the smooth coolness of the slippery scarves as they
rippled gently across my skin, just barely touching like the wings of a fairy.
 And the scent of old perfume – Ah! The sweet nostalgia of days gone by.

Oh, how I wish I still had those scarves now.

Guess I'll have to live with this coloring book that I've
created to commemorate those beautiful old scarves of days gone by,
the beautiful women who meant the world to me as a child, and my big
sister, Sandy, whom I will always love with all my heart!

Hope you enjoy,

Auntie V.

How Beautifully Leaves Grow Old

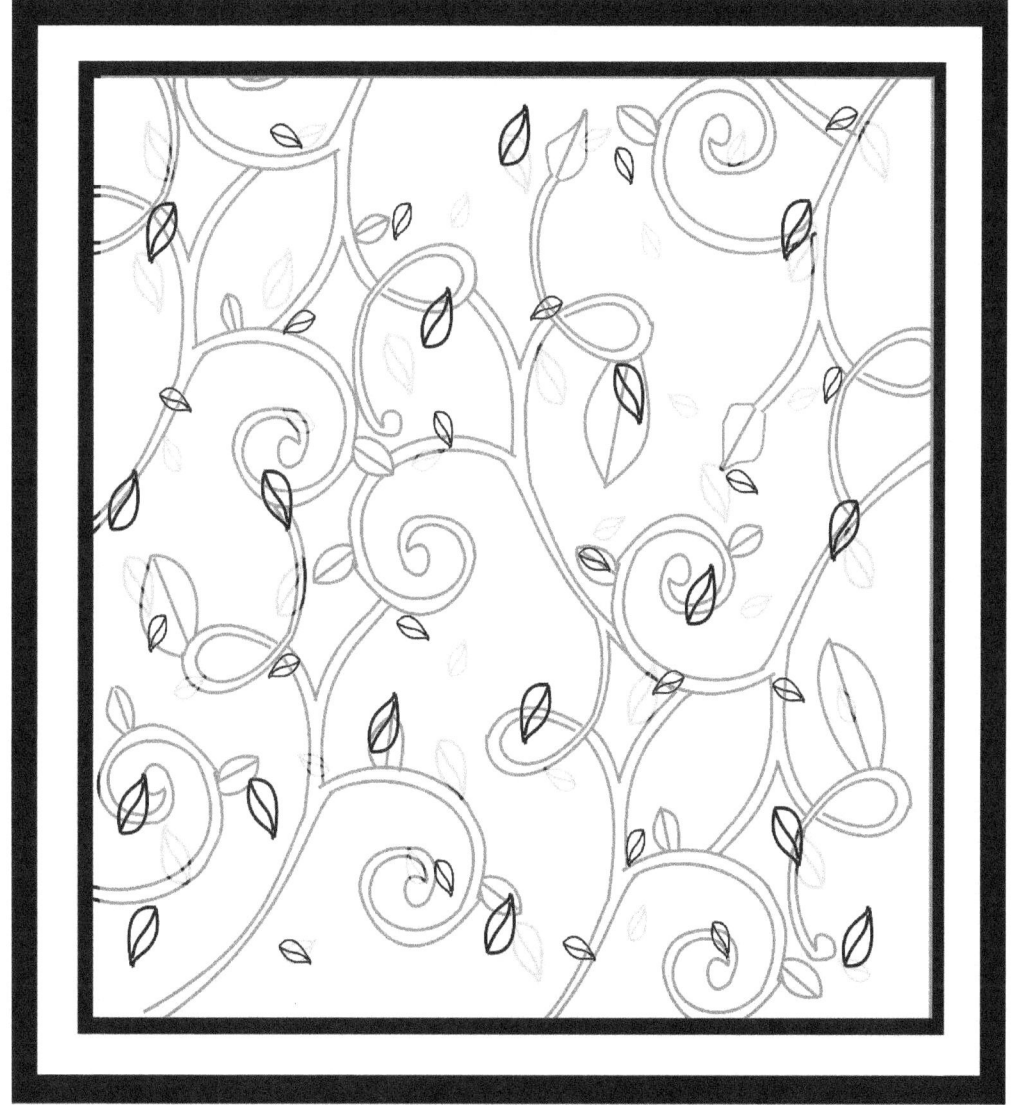

How Full of Light and Color are Their Last Days.

– John Burroughs

I AM GRATEFUL FOR THE

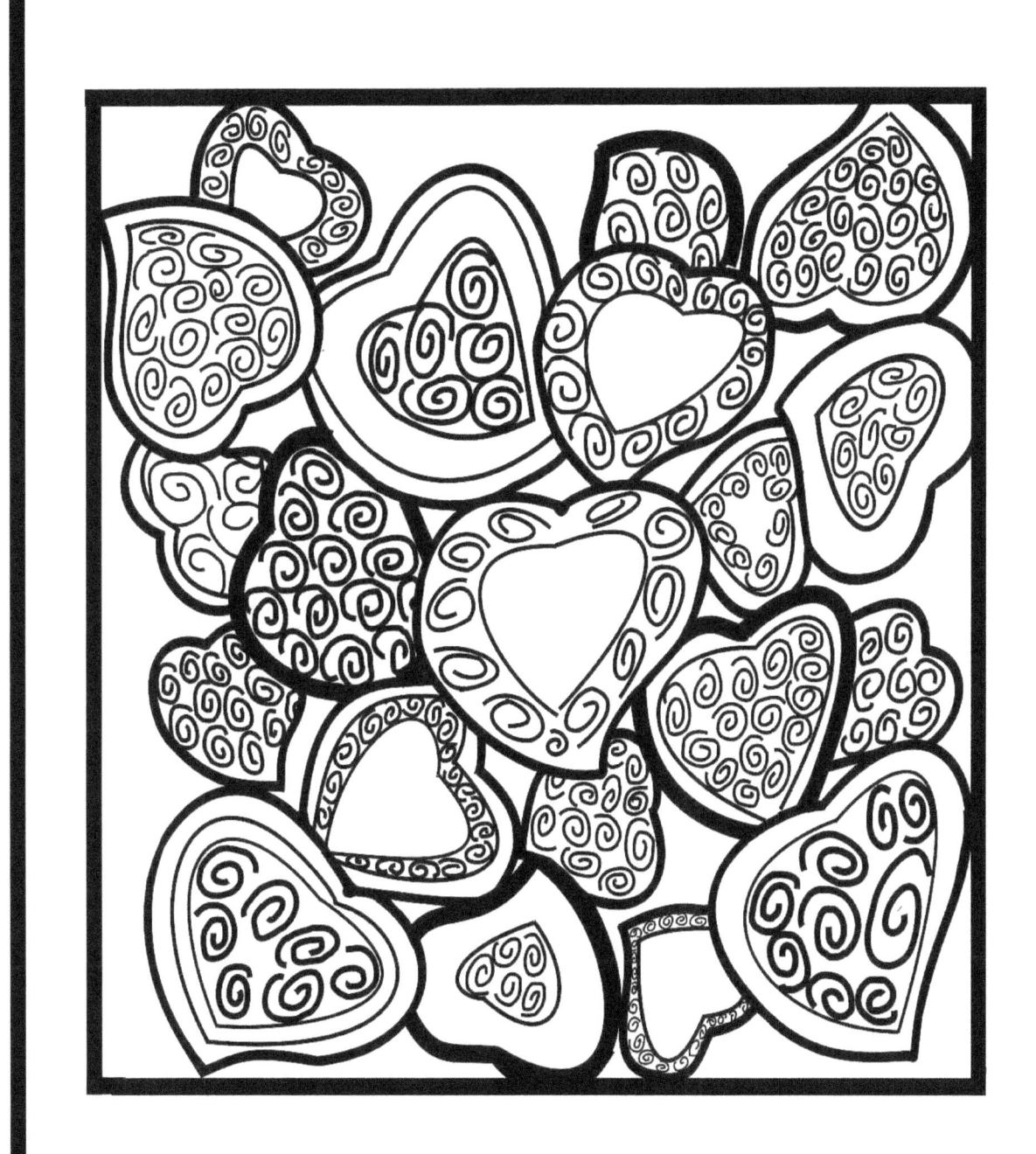

Love THAT IS AROUND ME

I ATTRACT
only GOOD things

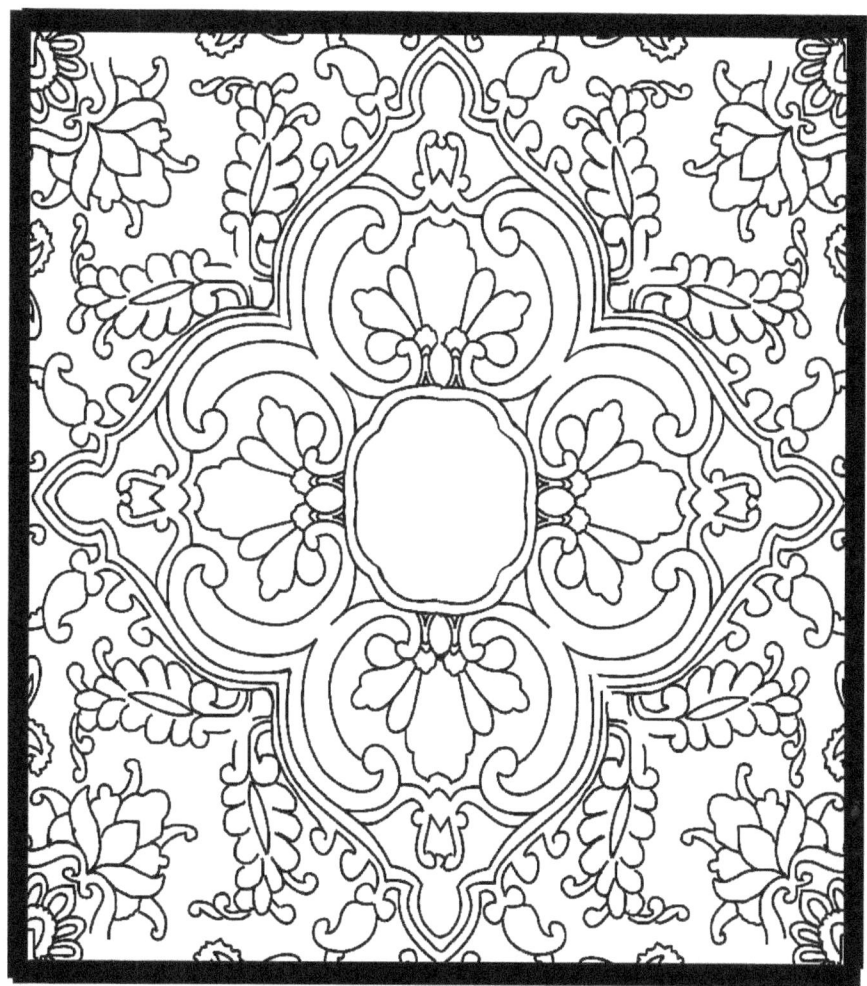

Into my Life

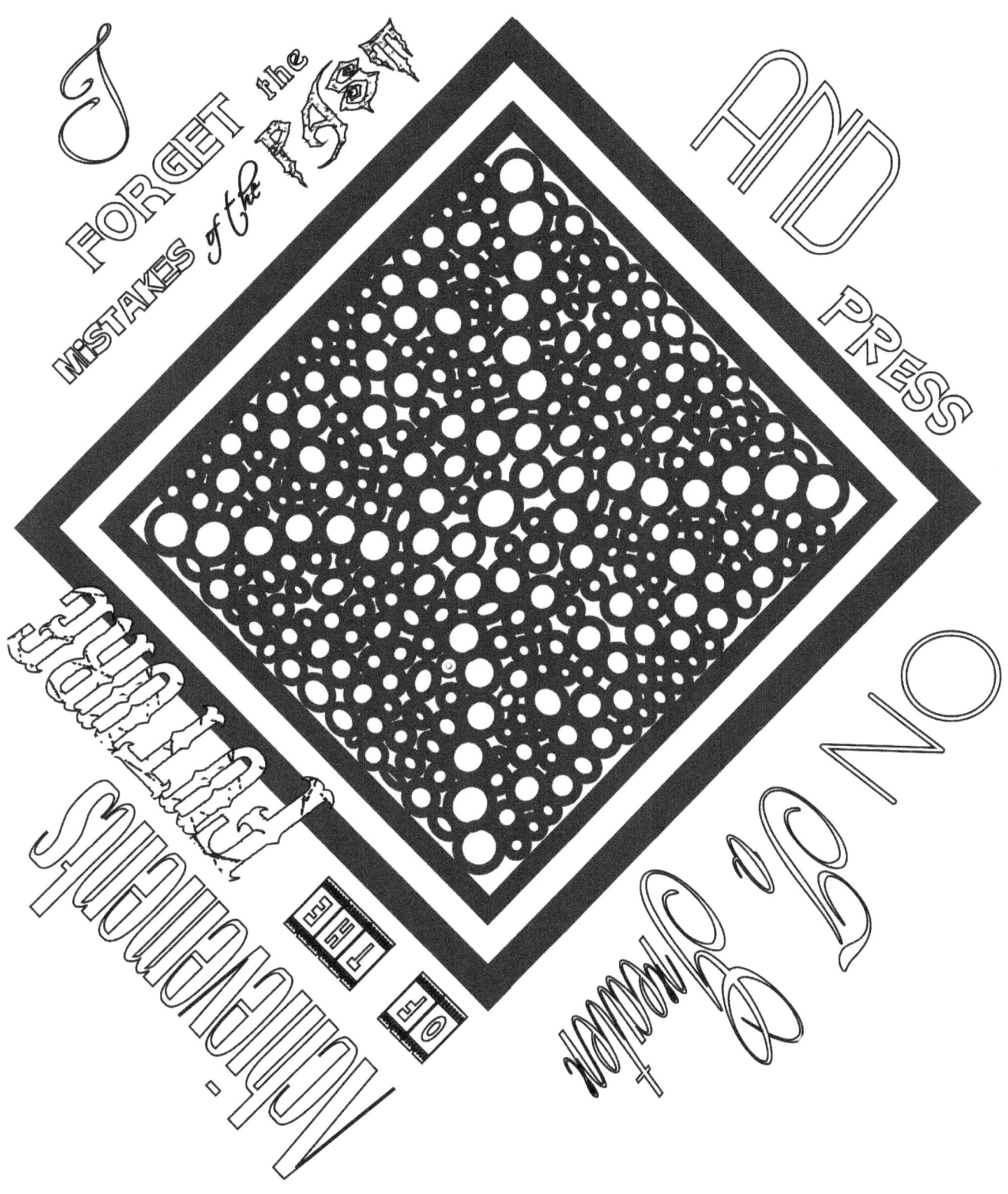

Good Things are Going To Happen

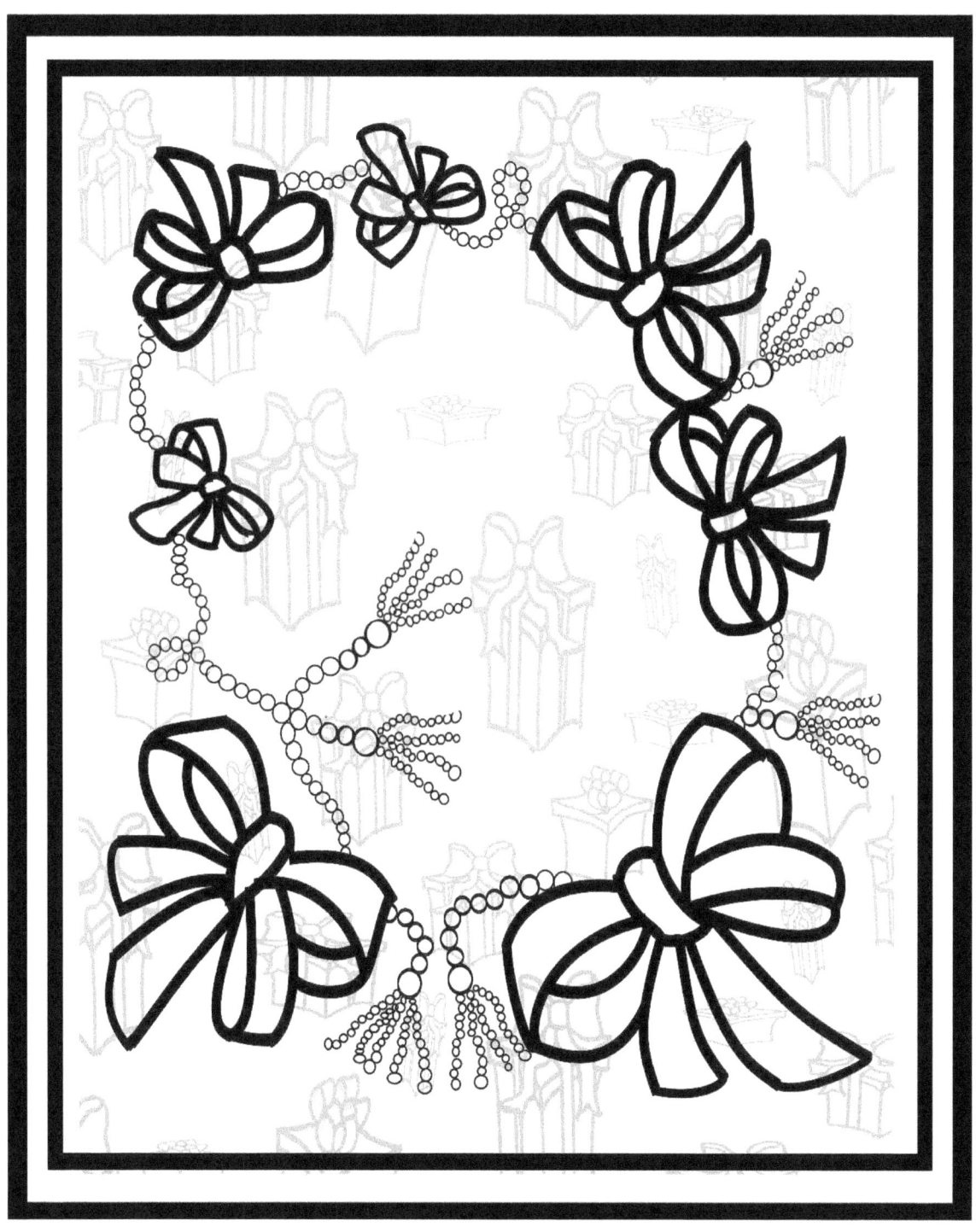

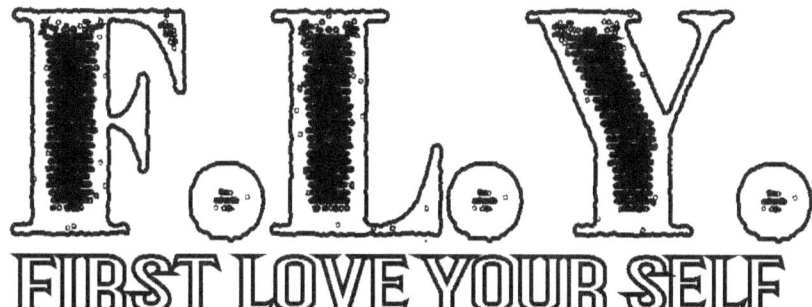

F.L.Y.
FIRST LOVE YOUR SELF

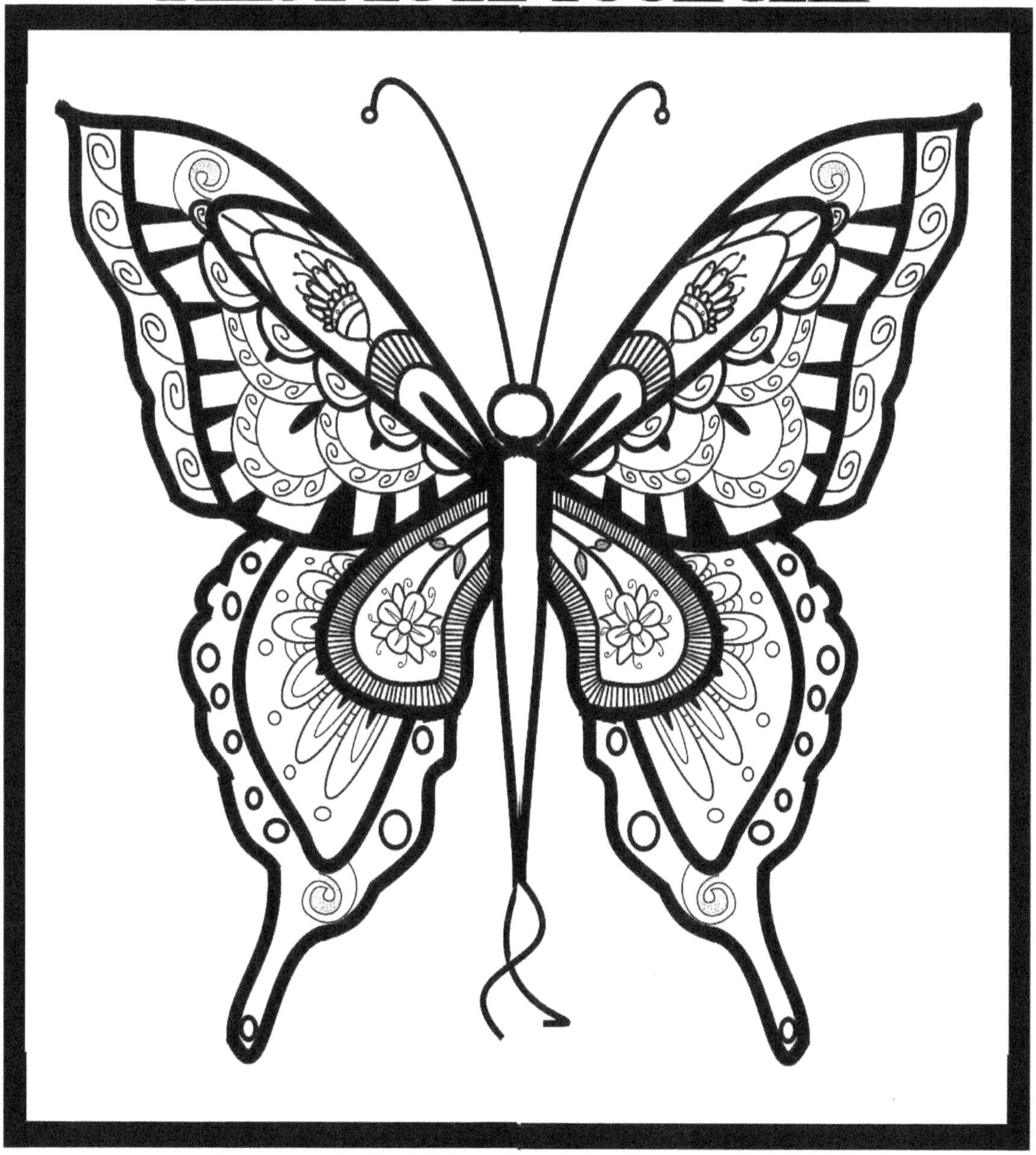

OTHERS WILL COME NEXT...

My thoughts are my reality....

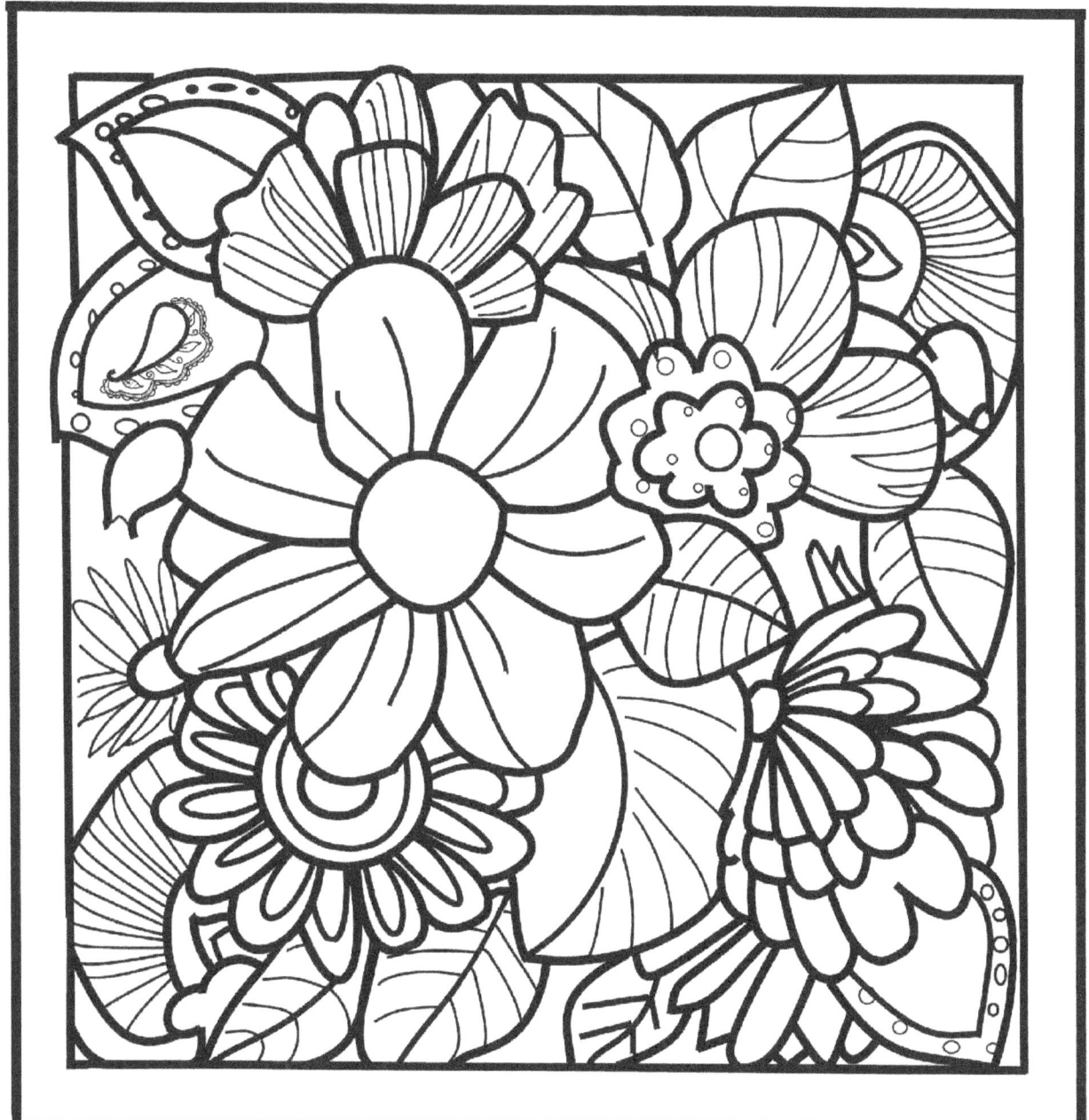

And I am thinking of a

Bright New Day.

IN THE END, IT'S NOT THE YEARS IN YOUR LIFE THAT COUNT, IT'S THE LIFE IN YOUR YEARS

Abraham Lincoln

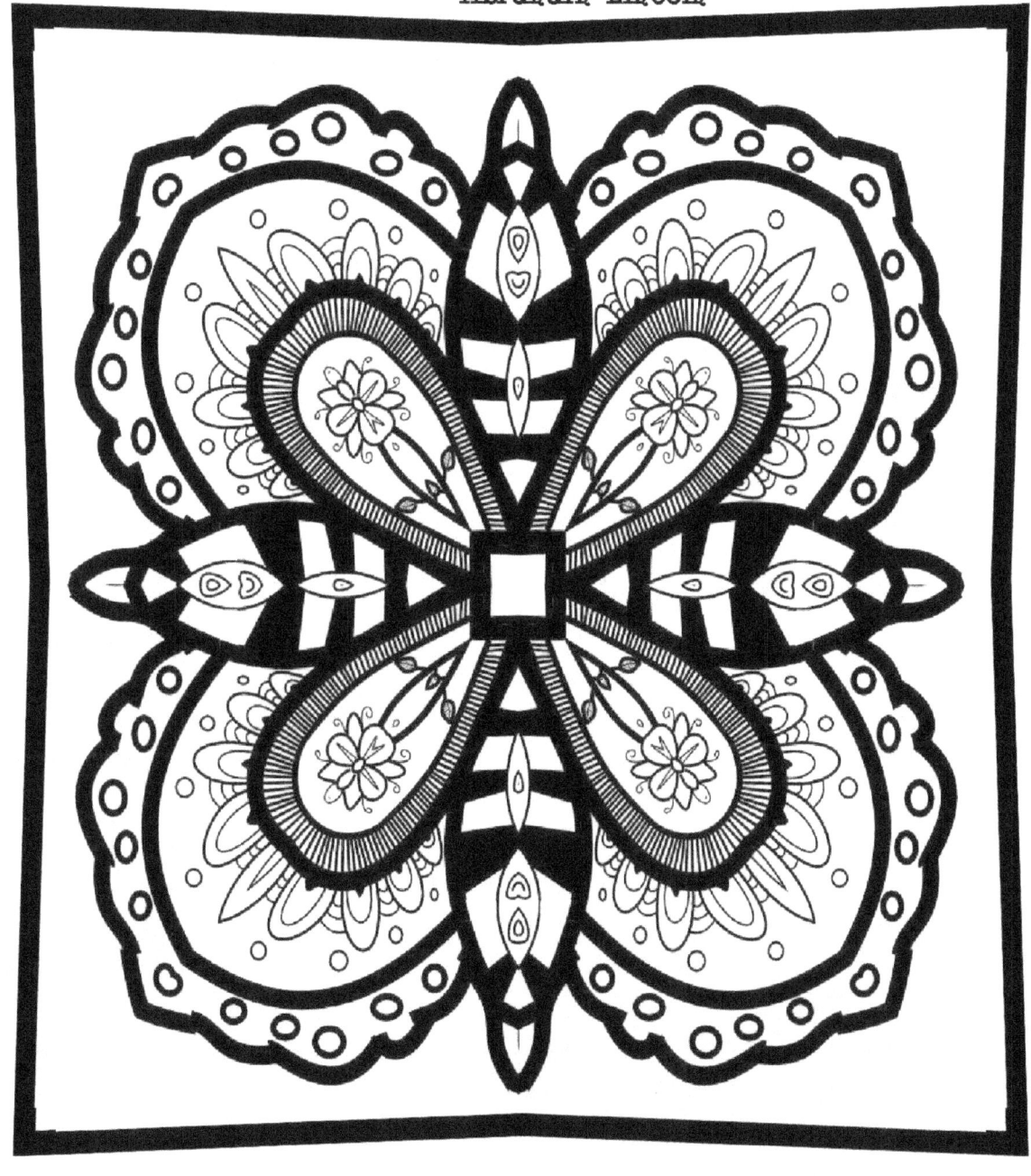

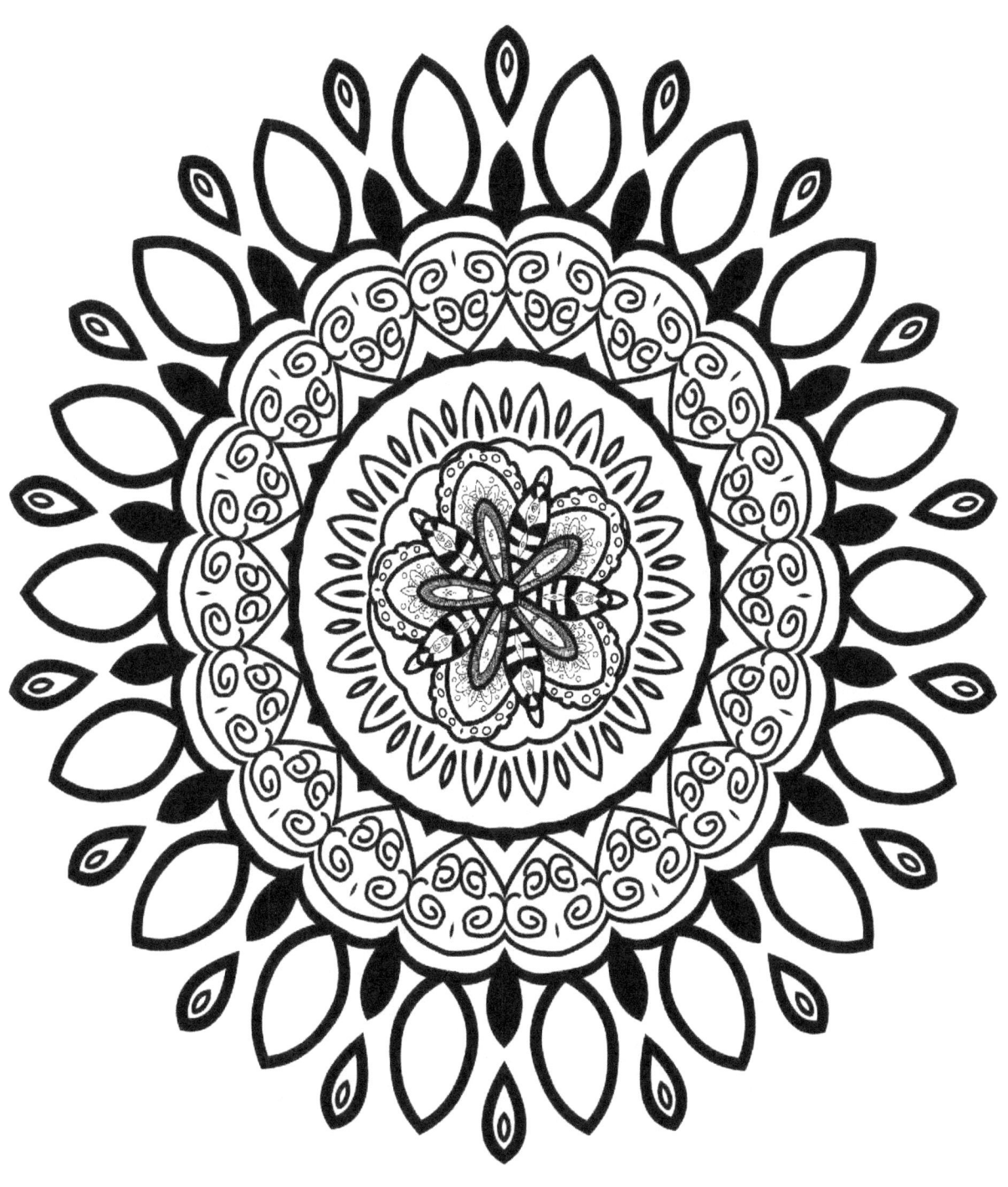

We gain the STRENGTH of the Temptation that we resist

Ralph Waldo Emerson

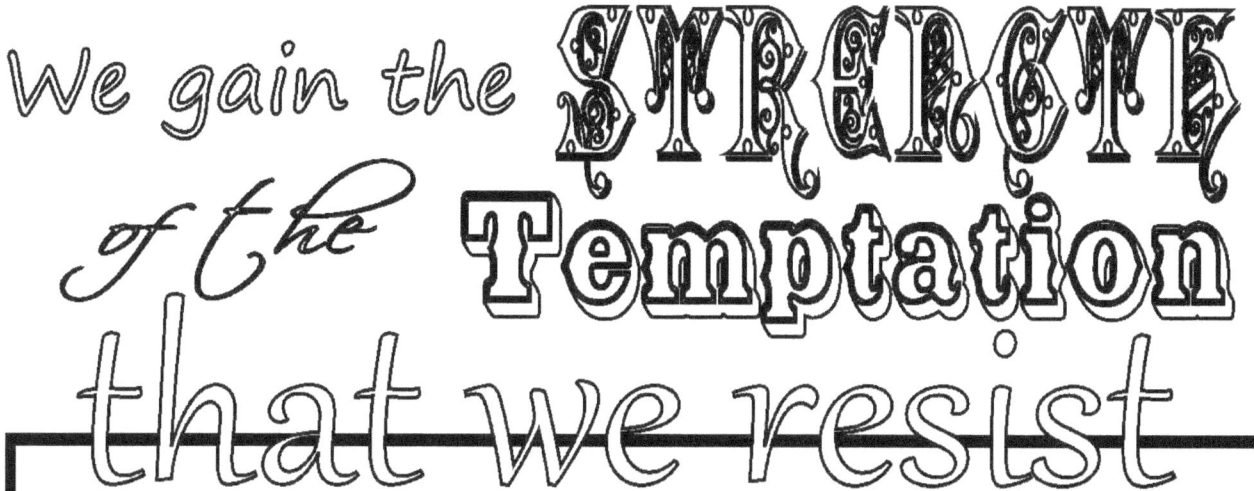

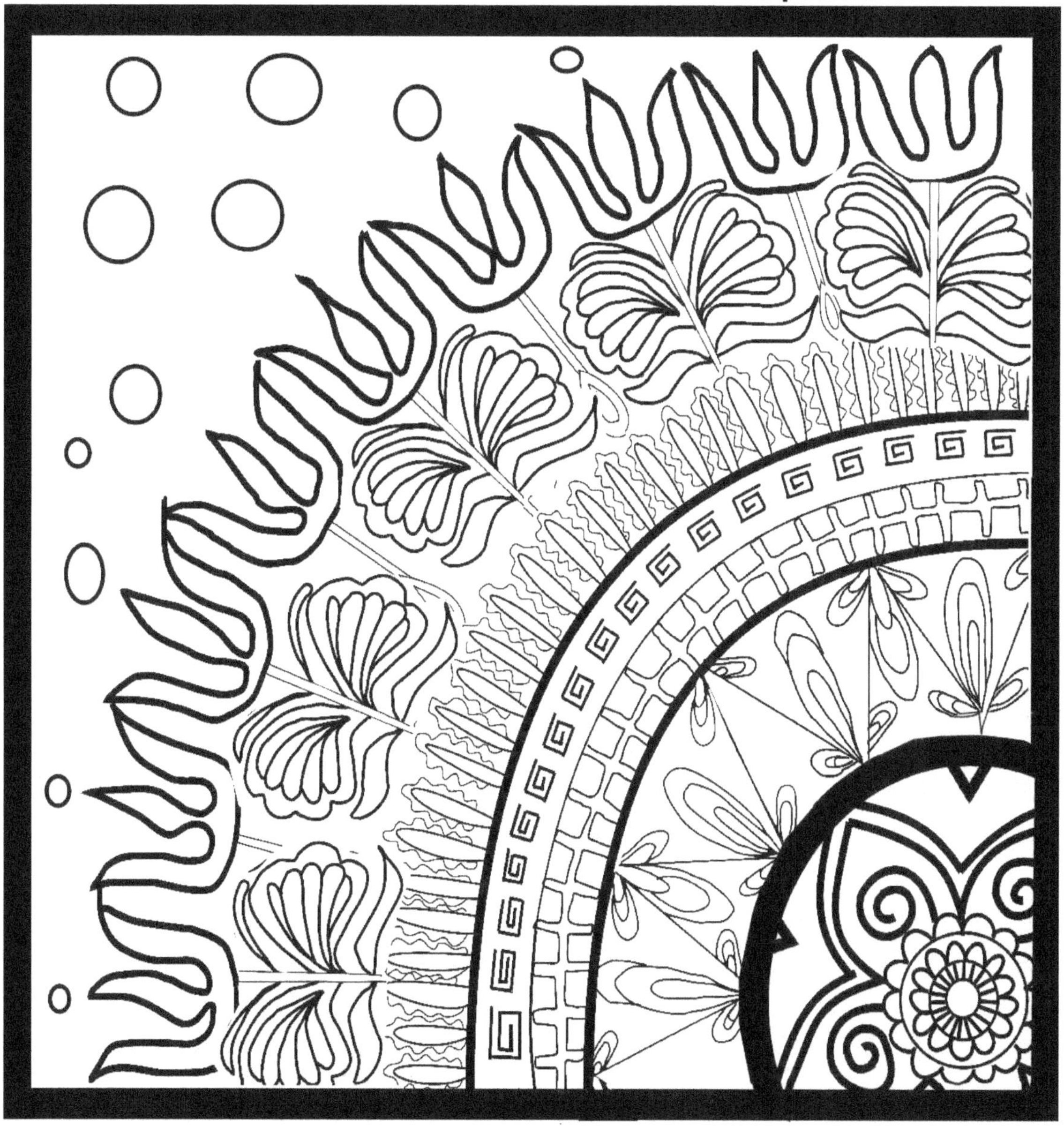

I am Bountiful, Blissfull and

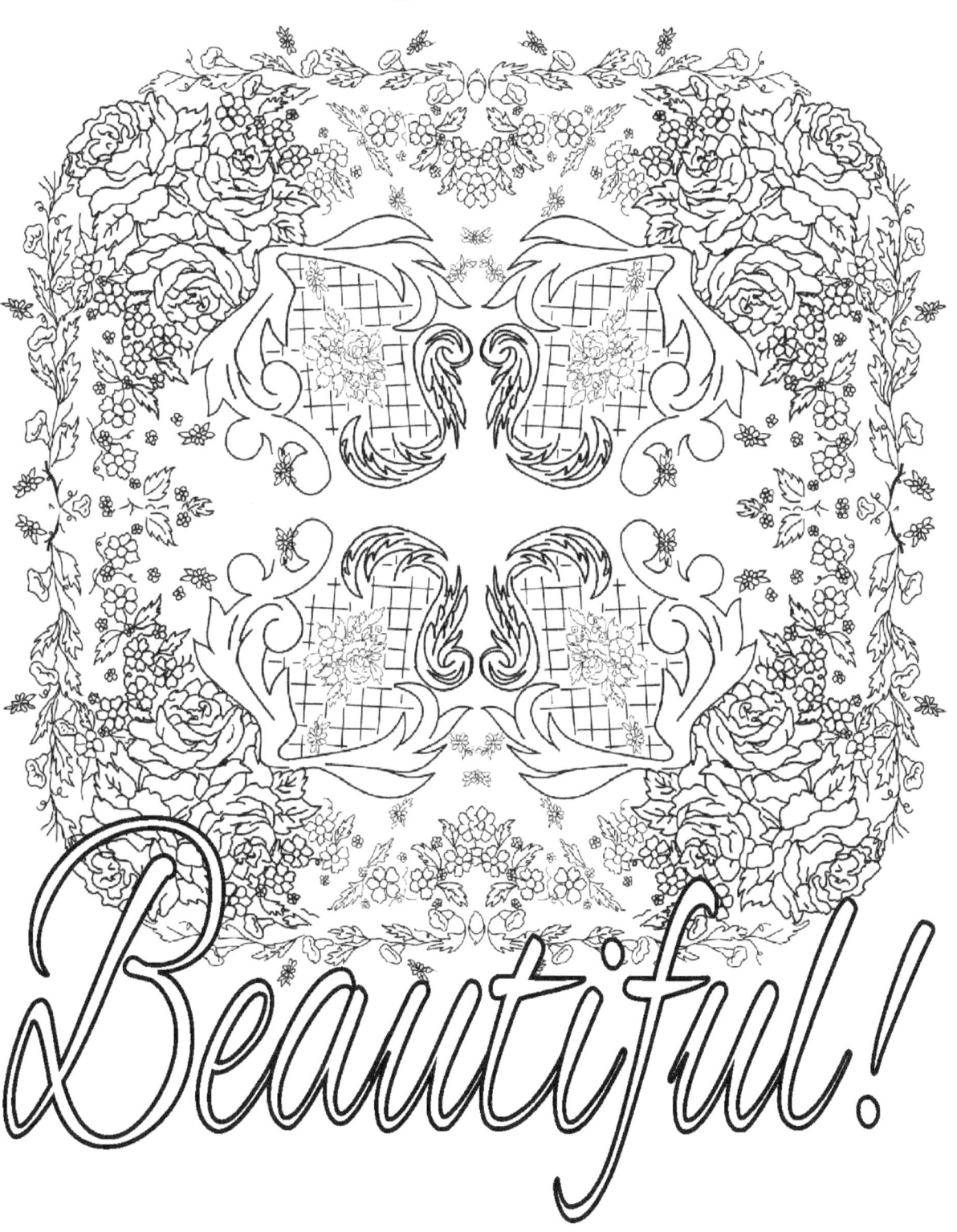

Beautiful!

I compare MYSELF ONLY To My Highest Self

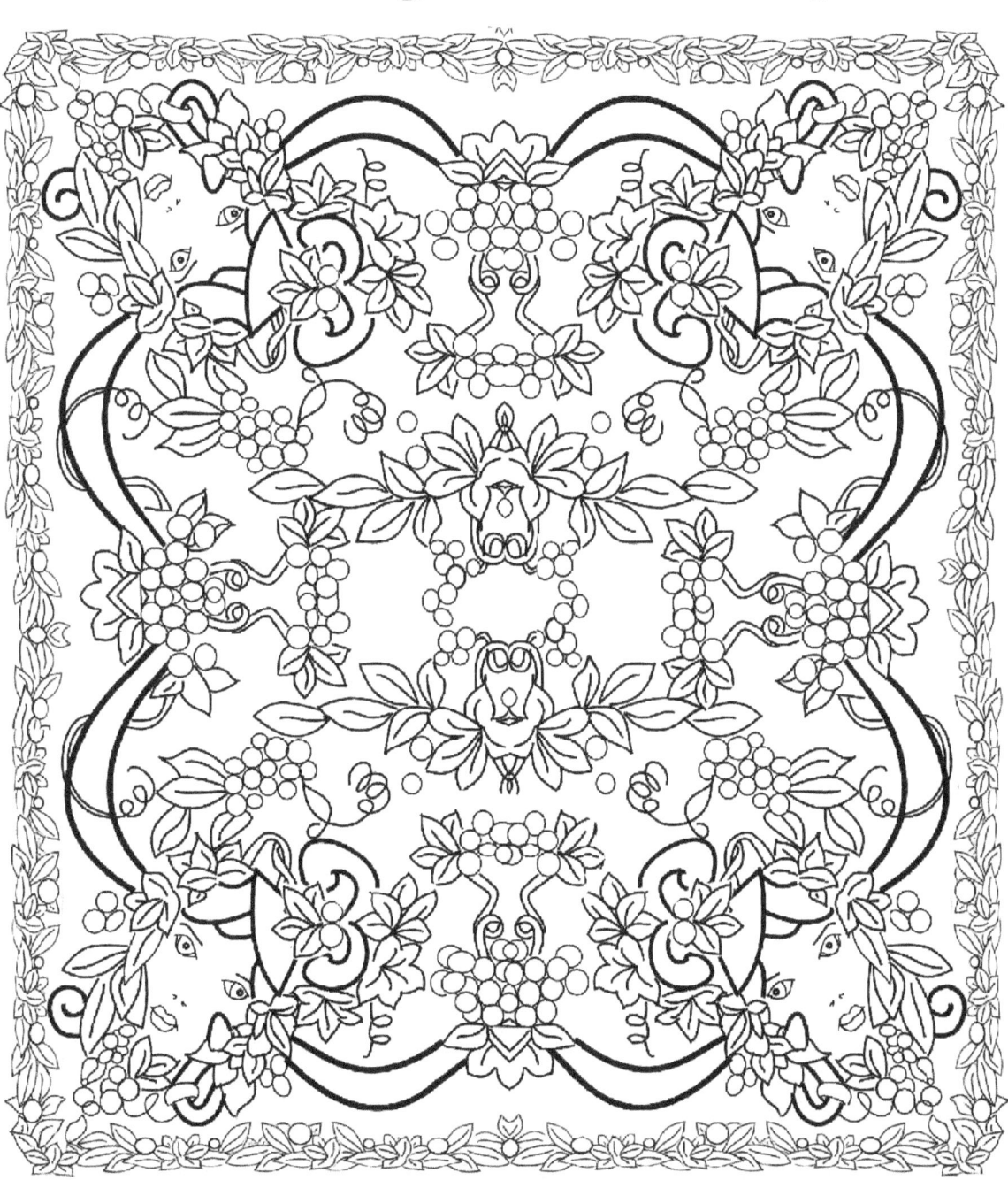

So if you wake up one morning and it's
a particularly beautiful day...
you''ll know we made it.

Robert Capa Sunshine

You Wait for an end, yet there is none...

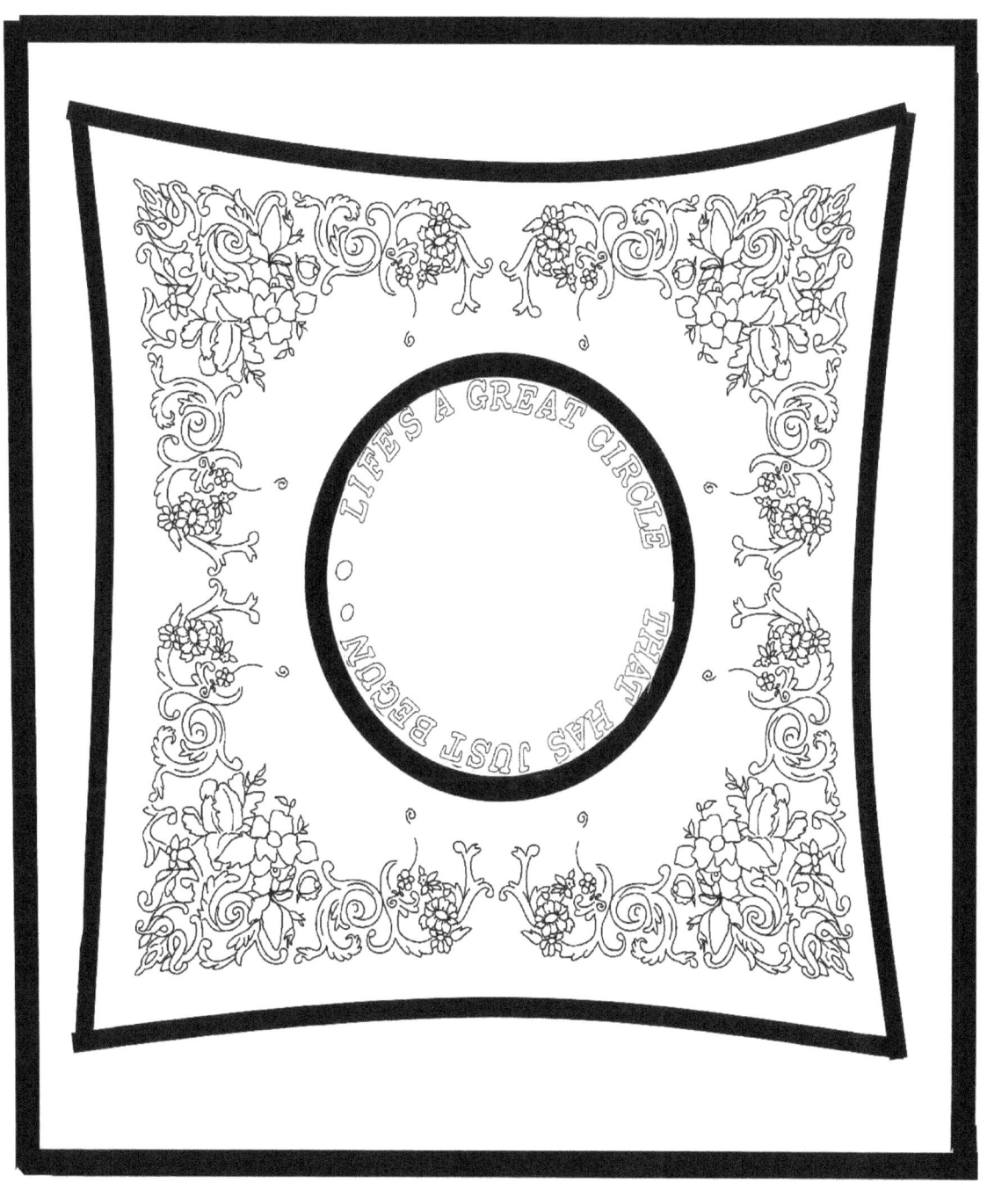

SOMETIMES *when you least* EXPECT IT...

Amazing THINGS CAN *and* Will

Happen.

It was June, and the world smelled of Roses.
The Sunshine was like powdered Gold over the grassy hillside.

Maud Hart Lovelace

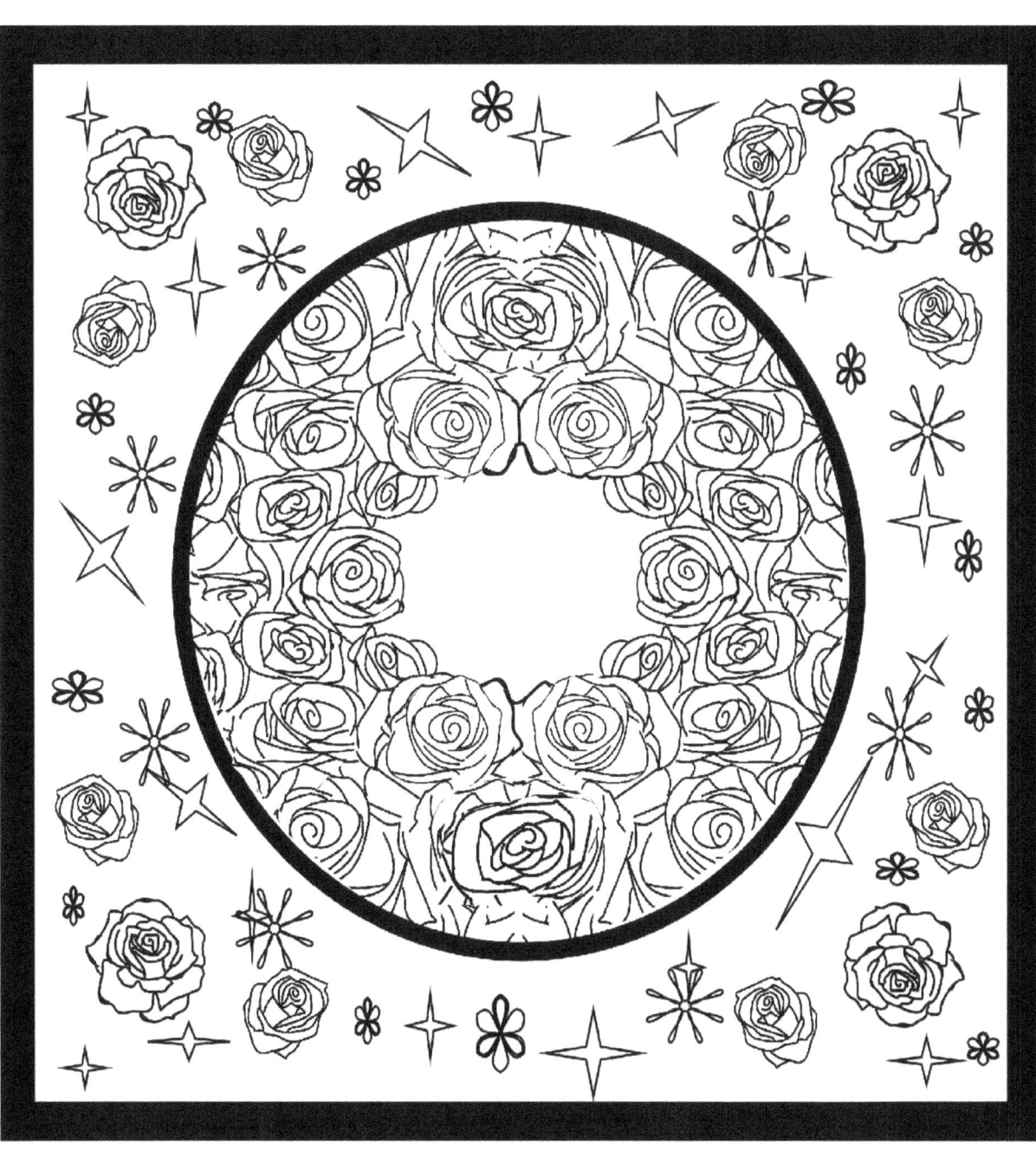

I am a Vessel of Ideas READY TO Burst!

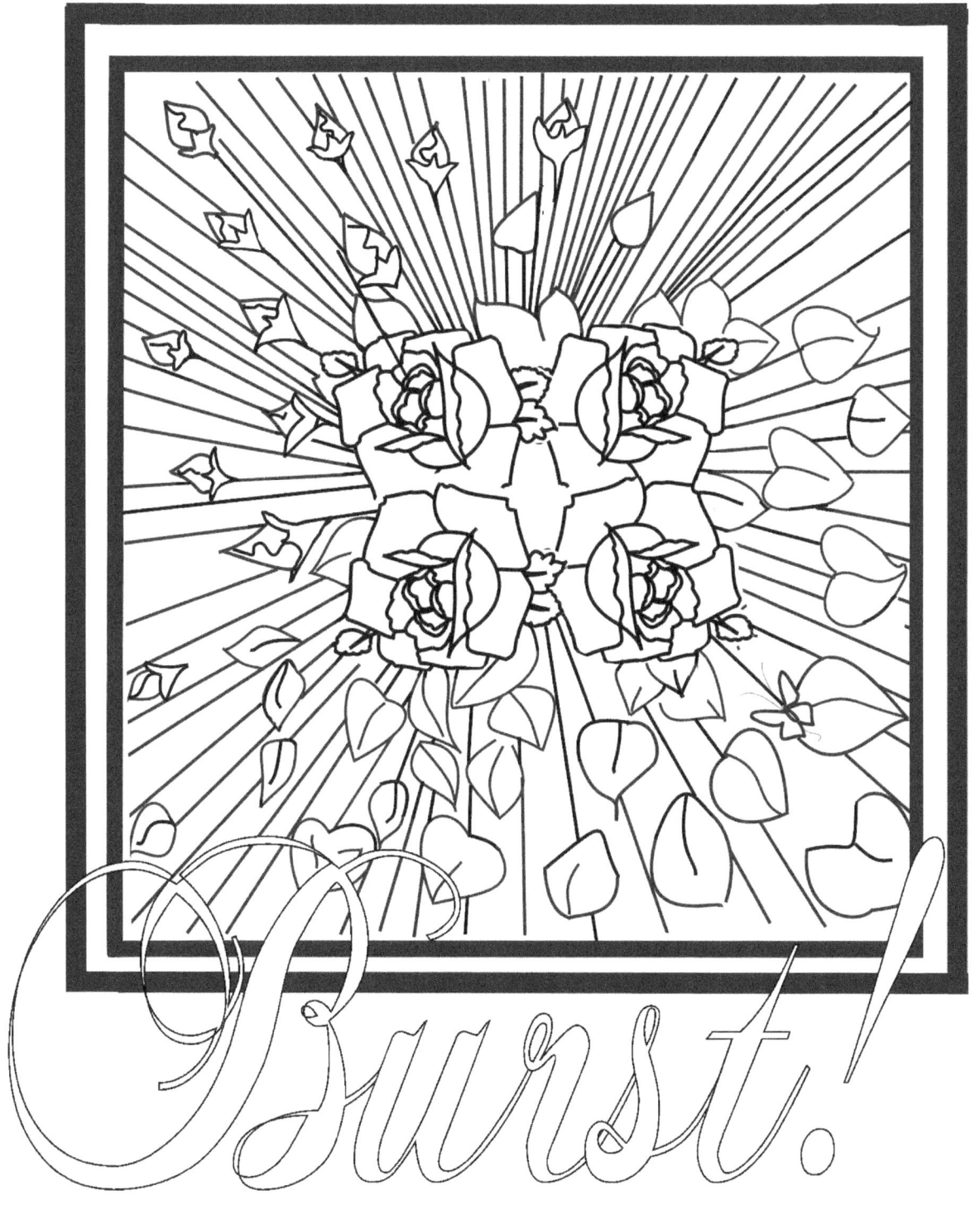

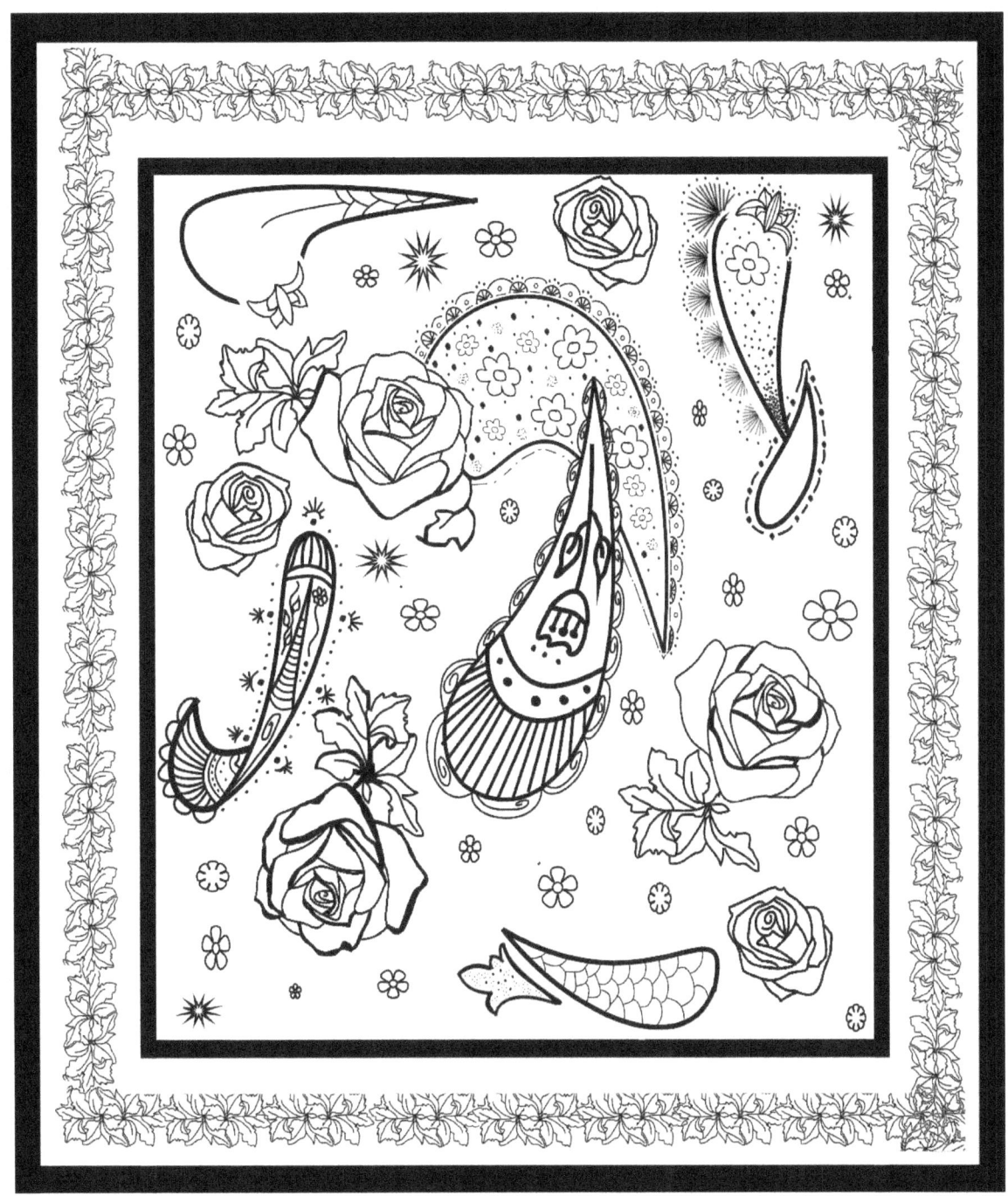

It just gets EASIER in that you become More You IN THE PROCESS.

Brad Paisley

IT'S NOT WHO YOU ARE
THAT HOLDS YOU BACK,
IT'S WHO YOU THINK YOU'RE NOT

Wonderfull things

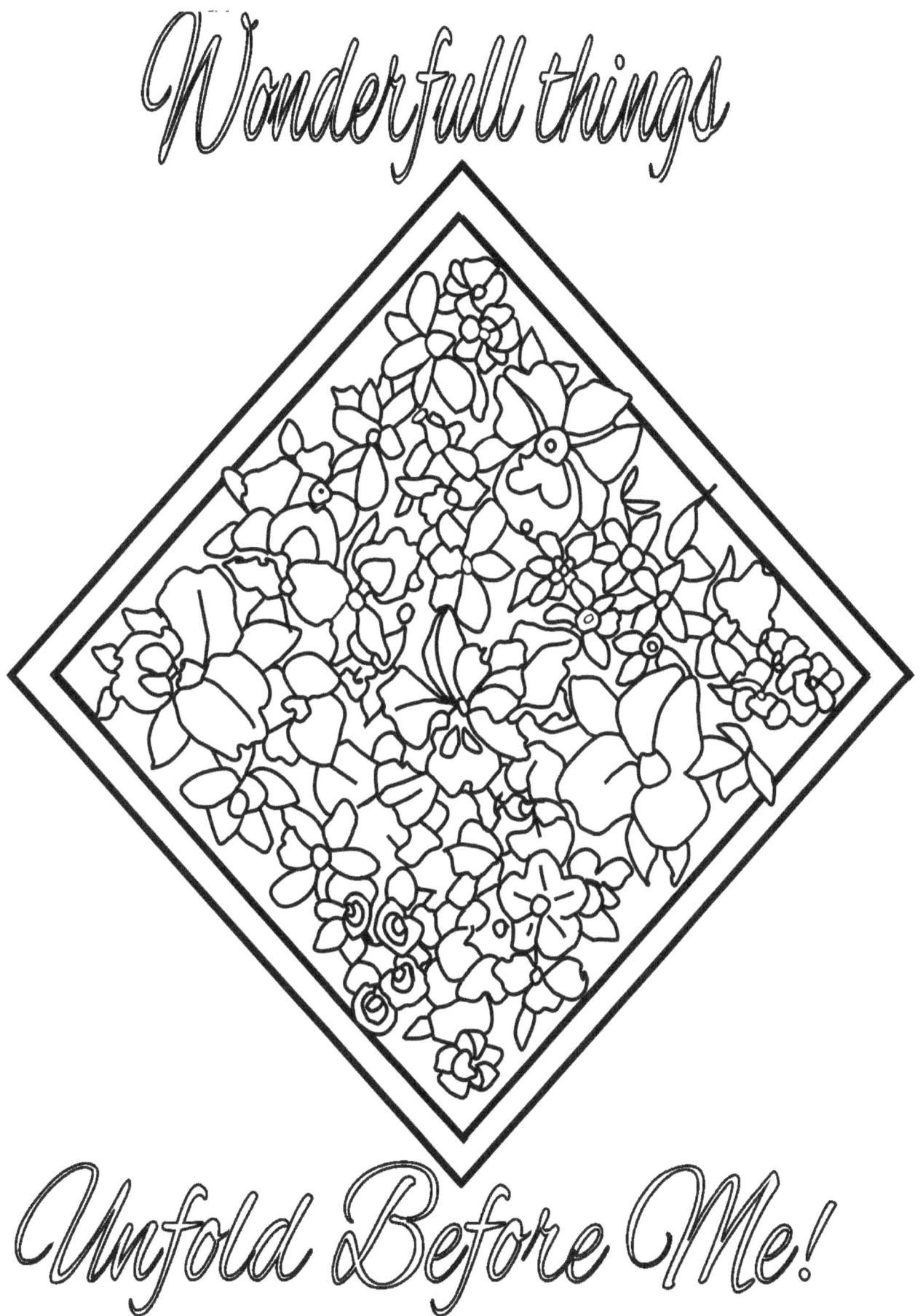

Unfold Before Me!

In the END,

We only REGRET

The CHANCES we didn't TAKE.

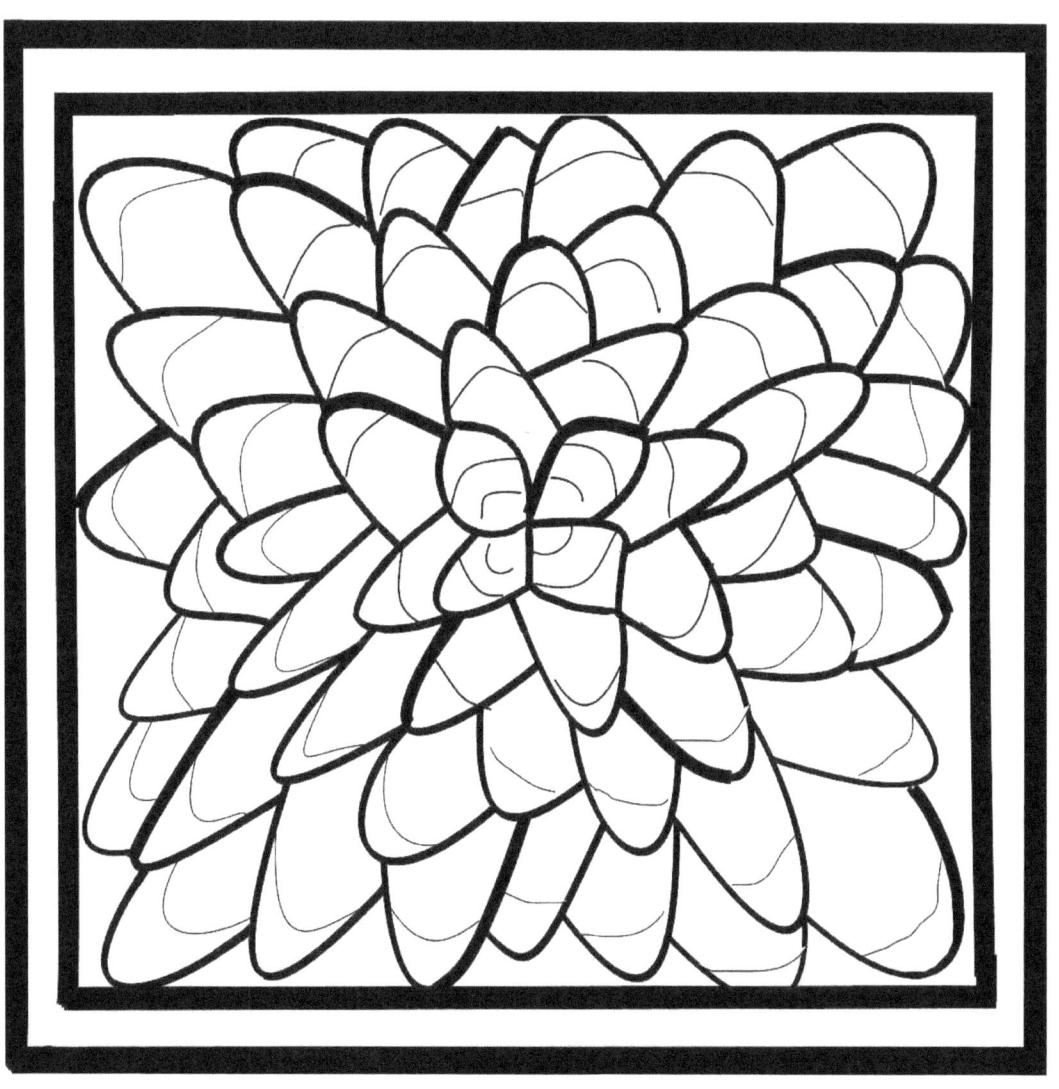

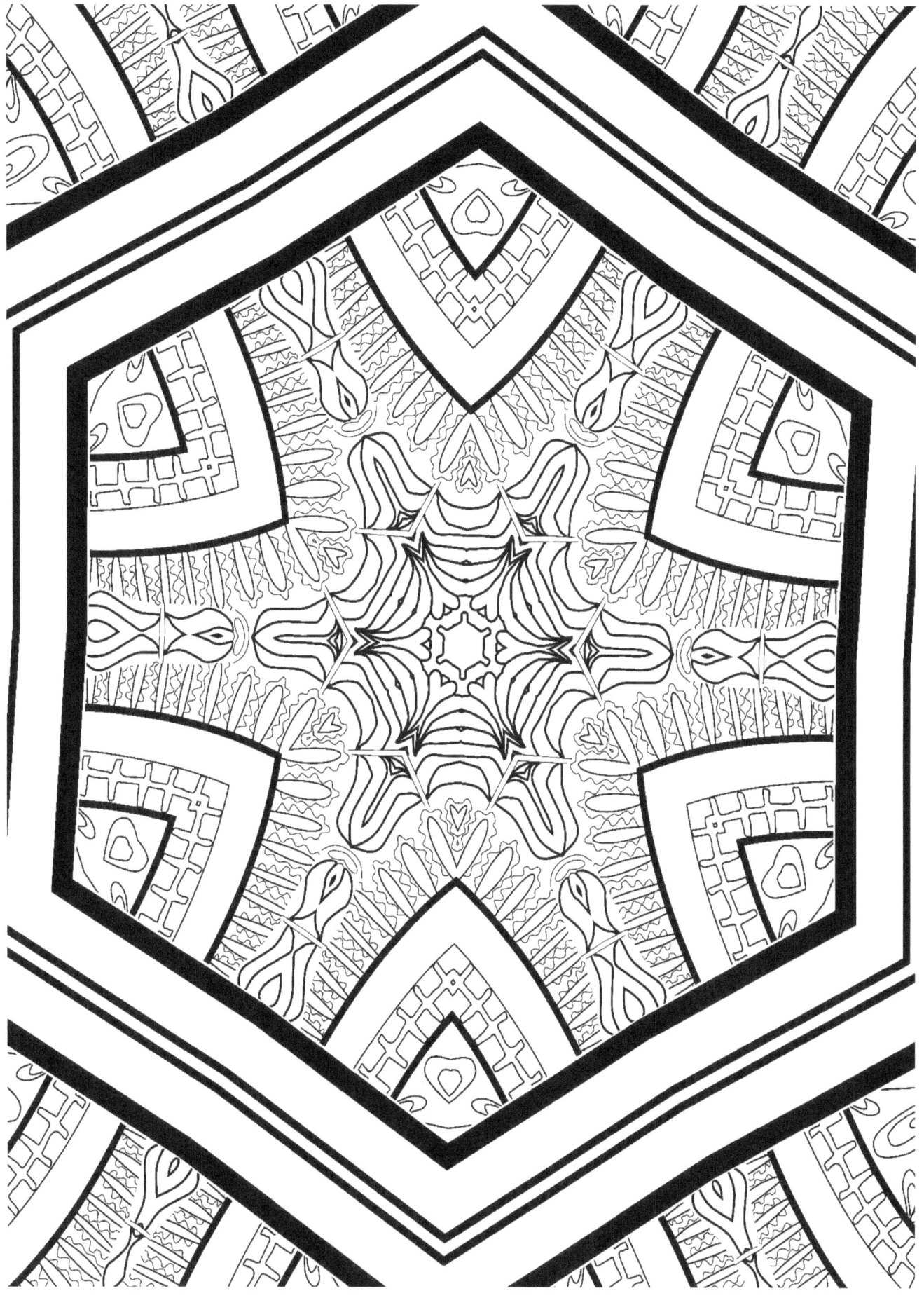

If you enjoyed Auntie V.'s Time Vault – Grannie's Scarves, please consider telling your friends or **posting a short review at this book's page at Amazon or on your Facebook page.** Word of mouth is a coloring book creators best friend and is much appreciated.

MORE COLORING BOOKS BY AUNTIE V.

AUTHOR CENTRAL: https://www.amazon.com/author/auntiev

Adult Coloring Book Valentine's Day: Coloring Books for Adults
Auntie V. 's Awesome Stress Relief Patterns Featuring Less Detail and Fresh
(Volume 2) Paperback – January 19, 2016

Auntie V's Faces of Dia de los Muertos: Adult Coloring Book
(Auntie V's Adult Coloring Books)
(Volume 1) Paperback – December 30, 2015

Visit Us Online

FACEBOOK: https://www.facebook.com/auntievscoloringbooksforadults/

TWITTER: https://twitter.com/AuntieVs   @AuntieVs

BLOG: https://auntievs.wordpress.com/

REDBUBBLE: http://www.redbubble.com/people/auntievs

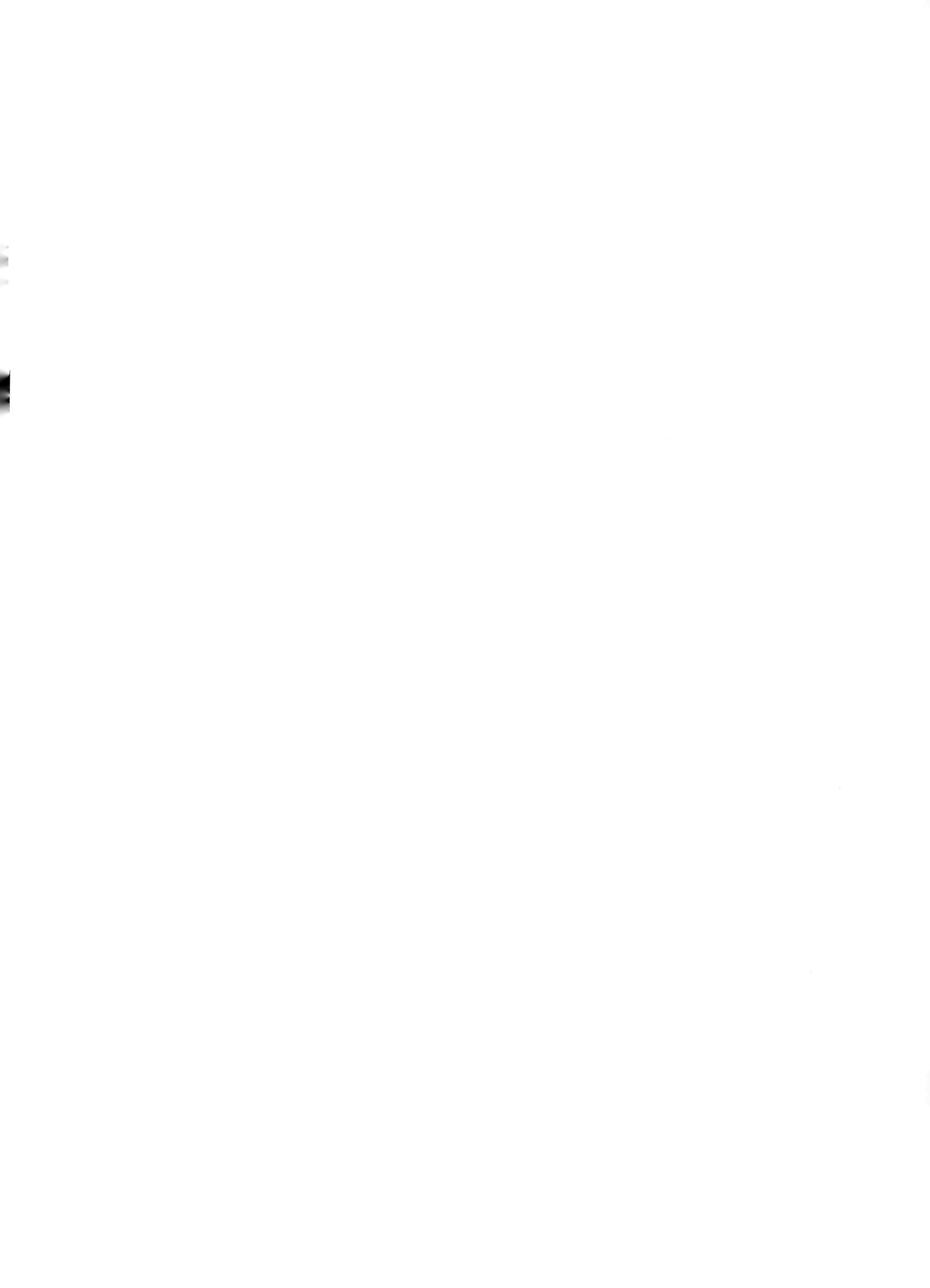